A FATHER'S LOVE

Written by
Gerald L. Jackson

Illustrated by
Lorena Soriano

Love is caring,
Love is kind,
this book was written
with you on my mind.

-GLJ-

Where do I begin to explain

how love comes from within.

A love that is so special, and so real,

it's just too hard to pretend.

You started out as an infant,

just small and innocent.

Watching you grow each day,

is worth every minute.

I love to watch you learn as you

see, hear, taste, and feel.

Take it all in, and don't let

fear keep you still.

It brings joy to my heart

to see you learn new things,

Continue to learn, and get

all of what life brings.

It hurts to see you

on days when you are sick,

But your strength shows me that you

can bounce back quick.

Remember, you were given two ears and one mouth for a reason,

So, be slow to speak and quick to hear and the reward will be pleasing.

I want you to ask questions, take
notes, and be prepared for any test.

Taking your time with your work,
will truly bring out your best.

Don't be afraid to challenge yourself,

whatever you start make sure you complete.

Your mind is your best weapon, and

a good education just can't be beat.

You will have friendships that

come and go,

But if you learn to love yourself first,

it will always show.

It's important to treat people the

way you want to be treated,

Never fake and with love

to show you mean it.

I love when you tell the truth,

it's much better than a lie.

Always be honest, because honesty is

worth more than anything you can buy.

Remember, love brings people
together and hate pushes people away.

Learn from each mistake,
to show others there is a better way.

You may not see me all the time

but like the wind I'm passing by.

You never know who is watching,

so always keep your head held high.

Love,
Your Father

To connect with the author visit:
www.geraldljackson.com

Add to your collection!
"A Father's Message" is the first book of the
series. Available on website or on Amazon.